Is Your Organization Invisible?

Five Must-Do Steps for Nonprofits to Become "Famous" to Donors, Volunteers, Funders and the Media

Richard Hoefer, Ph.D.
Shannon Graves

The Center for Advocacy, Nonprofit and Donor Organizations (CAN-DO)
University of Texas at Arlington School of Social Work
211 S. Cooper Street • PO Box 19129 Arlington, TX 76019

Find us online at www.uta.edu/can-do

This document is authored by and is the copyrighted material of Richard Hoefer and Shannon Graves.

© 2014 Richard Hoefer and Shannon Graves

Usage Guidelines
You do not have permission to copy, redistribute, or republish this work without the express written consent of the authors.

Find us online at www.uta.edu/can-do to access a constantly growing library of resources for nonprofit advocacy and human services management.

Table of Contents

Table of Contents 3
Foreword 4
Introduction: About this Report 4
Step 1: Develop a Plan to Raise Your Presence 7
Step 2: Produce Both Quality and Quantity of Content 13
Step 3: Be Current and "Evergreen" 17
Step 4: Create Variety 21
Step 5: Measure and Discuss Your Achievements 24
Wrap-up and Summary 28
BONUS Section: Maximizing Your Fame with Social Media Platforms . 30
Additional Written Resources 36
Can We Do Something More for You? 38
Learn More with Video Resources by CAN-DO 40

Foreword

When was the last time you used the Yellow Pages© to locate a particular type of store? When Rick was young, that's just how you found businesses and other organizations. We "let our fingers do the walking" by flipping pages until we came to the category we were looking for. Want to make some pottery or paint a picture? Look for the index entry "arts and crafts supplies". Were we in the mood to go bowling? Look up "bowling alleys". Pretty simple, though it wasn't always easy to tell which business was closest without a separate map.

Now, though, the internet has taken over. Our fingers do the walking anymore by typing in a question to a search engine. Almost every business has a website. If it has been optimized for search engine results, it comes up on the first page of results for important key terms.

Suppose you want to go bowling now. You can type in "bowling alley" plus a location, and get only the lanes closest to you. People then can click on a link and usually get all the information they're looking for, particularly about store hours, location and so on. In a sense, these businesses have become "famous" to people who want their products just by knowing how to maximize their search engine exposure.

But the internet revolution hasn't hit the nonprofit world fully. I know this is hard to believe, but a substantial number of nonprofits don't yet have a website.

Of those that do have websites, not all are well optimized for being high on the list of search engine results for important key words. These nonprofits are *not* famous: they can't be found by people who don't already know how to locate them. Think of how many donors aren't giving you money. Consider how many volunteers aren't showing up. Imagine how many foundations aren't finding out about your good work. Ponder how many journalists, bloggers and other reporters can't draw upon your expertise. Visualize the potential clients who can't find out about your services. In other words—realize how many opportunities you're letting slip by because you are not only, not famous, but you're close to invisible to all these important potential stakeholders, supporters, and even clients.

This report has been written to solve the issue of nonprofit invisibility. If you follow these steps and implement the ideas we share with you, soon this issue will be solved.

As with all the CAN-DO reports, we aren't anticipating that you'll be an expert in the topic after you've read through what we have to say. But you will know what to ask the people who are the true experts and you'll be able to make changes that will bring you to a higher level of fame—not fame for the sake of being famous, but shedding your invisibility so that your organization is better known, reaches more resources and achieves more of its mission.

Shannon

Rick

Introduction: About this Report

Is Your Organization Invisible?

Can people who want to find out about services like yours locate you quickly through a generic online search? Can foundations seeking for the best agencies in your field easily determine your value? Can media representatives locate you to get your take on important events in your area of expertise? Can potential clients searching for your services get the help they want?

In an increasingly technological world, your online visibility is one of the most important keys to getting the attention of donors, funders, volunteers, clients and information networks. People want to donate their money and time to organizations that are perceived as professional and high quality. Foundations increasingly reach out to nonprofits doing excellent work rather than waiting for funding applications. Media love organizations that know the latest information on developments in their field and are easily accessible. The fact is that people who want to use your services and support your cause must be able to find you and grow to trust you quickly and easily by using the internet or they will go elsewhere to have their needs met.

**People can't support you
if they don't know who you are.**

This short report will help you become "famous" by raising your online presence and getting the attention of important stakeholders who are currently looking for the top organizations in your field. Fame can be wonderful for your nonprofit, but the good kind of fame doesn't happen just by accident.

Think about your own behavior—how often do you search beyond the first page of results when you use a search engine? If you can get the information you want there, why would you painstakingly search through pages and pages of other listings? People looking for information about you, your services, and your field of expertise act the same way you do. They won't search past page one of the results any more than you will. Do you have a plan for landing (and staying) at the top of the heap through an active online presence?

For nonprofits, one of the best ways to become visible, valued and validated is by consistently sharing vibrant, in-depth and relevant information. Every human service nonprofit's website needs to be a showcase for its services, its specialized skills, and its valuable expertise. This report will help you begin to develop a credible online presence which supports your goals as an organization.

How to Get the Most from This Report

Many of the steps in the report will require some serious thought and strategic effort. Remember that "Rome wasn't built in a day!" Step 1 will help you develop a plan for how you can incorporate the other steps into your organization's daily activities. After reading through this report, return to Step 1 and create a realistic plan to achieve your big goals through manageable daily actions.

Start small, but start today!

While you can't do everything at once, take care not to dull your sense of urgency about getting your organization on the map. Every day that you're invisible is a day lost to donors, volunteers, clients and everyone else trying to help you achieve your goals. Remember that until you establish strong, healthy habits which ensure your online visibility, you remain invisible to those whose attention you need most. Start small, but start today!

Need More Guidance?

However you use this report, we hope that it will inspire you to think about your organization's work in a new way. We also hope that if you have any questions about the content here or if find yourself facing challenges that are bigger than the scope of this report, that you will reach out to CAN-DO to have your questions addressed and learn how training and technical assistance from CAN-DO (www.uta.edu/can-do) may be able to help YOU. Now, let's list the Five Must-Dos to make your organization famous! (We'll cover them in detail later on.)

1. Develop a plan to raise your presence.
2. Produce both quality and quantity of content.
3. Be current and "evergreen".
4. Create variety.
5. Measure your achievements.

Step 1: Develop a Plan to Raise Your Presence

As you have already learned, individuals, foundations and media representatives are most likely to become familiar with you when you appear on the first page of results for important search terms. If you're not on the first page of listings, your goal should be to move up over time, so that your knowledge and services are in the top ten results on Google, Bing, and other major search engines. If you are already there, congratulations! You can use this report to maintain healthy habits that will keep you at the top.

The first step in raising your visibility is developing a strategic plan which clearly defines: (a) where you are currently at, (b) where you want to be, and (c) how you plan to get from point A to point B. Because your online presence will be constantly responsive to your efforts, your plan should include ongoing actions to which you are committed daily, weekly, monthly, and annually. Be specific about what is going to happen, who is going to be responsible for doing it, and when the action will start. On the next page, we provide a helpful template for writing out your plan.

If you're not yet sure *what* to write, don't worry. In Steps 2 – 5, you will learn specific strategies that can help you increase your online presence as part of your overall strategic plan. We recommend reading on and returning to Step 1 with fresh ideas about how to incorporate the knowledge gained from this report into your plan for internet stardom!

Becoming Famous

Creating an Online Presence Plan

Our Goal: To achieve or maintain a front page place on Google, Yahoo, Bing and other search engines.

Your plan to achieve this goal has, at this point, two actions for you to take.

Action 1-1: Determine what you want to be known for.

This may be easy for you to determine, or it may be difficult, but you must choose to focus on a limited set of terms. Most likely, you have one or a few services that are most important to your mission. You'll want to focus on these.

Let's choose a nonprofit's mission statement and other information to examine as an example without naming the organization, which is located in Dallas, Texas. These lines come from their website. Read through these short paragraphs and write down what are the important elements that they might want to be "famous" for.

Unnamed Nonprofit, Inc. offers drug and alcohol detoxification treatment plus comprehensive residential and outpatient programs with counseling, recovery supports, and education about the disease of addiction and the life skills needed to return to a productive life. We also provide psychiatric and dual diagnosis programs.

Our mission is to promote the development of positive behavioral health and independence for individuals and families caught up in the cycles of substance abuse and addiction, criminal behavior and mental illness.

Becoming Famous

We offer:
1. Residential and outpatient drug and alcohol treatment, detoxification, group and individual counseling, and social services for men and women ages 18 and above
2. Mental health assessment, counseling and crisis stabilization services
3. Medication supported outpatient treatment for opiate dependent men and women
4. Family Support Groups and Parenting Groups
5. AA Groups and Recovery Support Services
6. Continuing education and supervision for professional counselors and licensed healthcare practitioners

What are five terms that you think this organization would want to be found for in a search on the internet? (Feel free to think of additional terms, as well).

1. _____
2. _____
3. _____
4. _____
5. _____

As you looked over the organization's information, some of the terms that came to your mind might have been:

1. _Substance abuse treatment Dallas_____
2. _Detoxification Dallas_____
3. _Mental health assessment Dallas_____
4. _Opiate dependence treatment Dallas_____
5. _Family support groups Dallas_____
6. _Continuing education counselors Dallas__

7. _Parenting groups Dallas_____
8. _Dual diagnosis treatment Dallas_____
9. _Addiction treatment Dallas_____
10. _Adult addiction treatment Dallas_____

Note the importance of adding a location to the search term. Because this is a treatment facility in Dallas, the terms to be most known for should also be connected with that area. Google and other search engines generally keep track of the location of the person typing the query. The results generally are kept to that area, if possible. Remember, the goal of Google is to give you its best guess as to what information you wish to find and most people want to find services nearby.

With a list such as this, the nonprofit is now ready to plan how to become known for these terms and phrases, which are the sorts of terms people will type into search engines.

Action 1-2: Develop content about these terms.

Content, in this context, means just about anything that can go on the internet. Primarily we think about your website, but it also includes any related blogs, reports, videos, podcasts, interviews, etc. that have the terms you've identified in them. Each of these types of content have some different subtleties, but at this point, that is less important than if you create a lot of valuable information on these terms.

It is best to develop a content creation plan so that you have a schedule and a set of topics (key words) that you will have content about. It is not too much to have a new article of 400-500 words per week put on your website. The genius of this approach is to realize that you can use the same content on different platforms. The information from a new website page can also be turned into a blog article, a new posting on Facebook, an infographic or image on Pinterest, a podcast topic, and so on. Scheduling these as part of the work week keeps this vital task from becoming something that can be forgotten about or put aside.

Action 1-3: Put your content on your website and spread links to your new content to your contacts and other dissemination venues.

Google and other search engines constantly do two things: search the internet for new information relating to specific search terms (such as the terms listed earlier) and locate links from one website to another (these are called backlinks). You need to take advantage of knowing what, in general, the search engines are doing to become more famous in your chosen areas.

By having the terms in the content that are on your site, you increase the chances that your organization's website will be on the first page of results for those terms. Now, search engines have learned to avoid websites and pages with terms "overly packed" with the same phrase or word, but if the content reads like a normal English-language document, you are unlikely to be penalized for having the key word too often.

Remember that, when properly tagged, each page on your website, every video on YouTube, every article in an article depository, is a separate opportunity to be indexed in the search engines. Frequently, in fact, almost always, when people search for specific information that relates to content that you have on your website, they will go to the page with the information, not to the home page of your site.

That is why you can have several different spots on the first page of the search results if you have connected and authoritative content on your terms on separate pages and in different venues. Even if the content is similar, a search engine result can refer to your webpage as #1 and a YouTube video your organization developed as #2. A special report written by your CEO and posted on LinkedIn can also link back to your organization and be ranked #3 in the Google results.

Action 1-4: Spread the word and get backlinks to your material.

In addition, you want to encourage the readers of your content to include the web page address on their websites and blogs, too. The reason this is important is because Google sees people referring to your website and takes this as a sort of vote in favor of the content linked back to. If you have a large number of sites that "vote" in favor of linking to your site rather than creating their own content on the topic, Google moves your content up in the search results. The higher up you are, the more likely you'll be on page one, where the largest percentage of people will connect you to that information. This is how you stop being invisible and become famous!

Step 2: Produce Both Quality and Quantity of Content

Some people will argue that quality content is more important than quantity; others will say the opposite. The truth is you should strive for both. Search engine rankings are based on the quantity, quality, and relevance of your content, and the amount of "successful" traffic visiting your site. Successful traffic means people who click on your site and actually find what they are looking for rather than clicking the back button a moment or two later. It is also related to search engines finding backlinks to your content, as discussed earlier.

A high volume of content is the first step to building an online reputation, as it gives searchers lots of opportunities to come across your material. A simple website which only contains information about your purpose, location, and services will only draw visitors who are already looking for you and the specific services you offer. Adding content in the form of articles, blog posts, audio and video recordings, and other links increases the number of purposes for which people may visit your site as well as the number of keywords and search terms through which they may find you. Consider adding the following types of content to your site:

- General information about the problems you address
- General information about the type of services you provide
- Research that supports the need for you and your approach
- Spotlights on staff, volunteers, donors, and clients (if appropriate)
- National and community resources related to your field
- "Unrelated" information of interest to your target populations

As you increase the quantity of content, be cautious of posting the same content in multiple locations on your site. Overlapping information between different pieces is great, and provides a reason for visitors to trail from one content page to another, but copying and pasting the same text in multiple places may well result in search engines downgrading the ranking of your material.

Quality and quantity of information are both important.

Committing to producing a large volume of high *quality* content means you will receive more successful visits to your site, that is people who find what they are looking for. It does your organization little good to win visitors who arrive and are unable to quickly find what they are looking for. Such visits decrease your search result status. Perhaps more importantly, quality content means that people who land on your page are more likely to find your organization a reputable source of valuable information. As a result, visitors will be more likely to bookmark your site and return again in the future or direct others to you as a trusted resource.

One of your primary goals is to publicize your organization's name as a leading source of information in your field. Make sure your name and links to other relevant information are prominent on all pages of your site, so that your knowledge is easily linked back to you and your fame-worthy reputation.

Having both high quality and high quantity of content means that you will be listed higher on the page of search engine results for your key terms and you will take up more of the spots on the first page. This is what you are aiming for—more content means more viewers. And if what you produce is all good quality, the people finding your content are going to be happy to consume it. This, in time, will lead to higher page rankings, an increased reputation and "fame" for your organization within your field. Your organization will be visible, recognized, and sought after, exactly what you are aiming for.

Action 2-1: Make it someone's job.
Assign someone the job responsibility of maintaining the content creation schedule created Step 1, Action 2. If no one is responsible for it, the content won't be created. Everyone is busy and there is always a reason to skip the task of writing content. Make sure someone is in charge of getting this done.

Action 2-2: Make it everyone's job.
While you want to take Action 2-1 so that the overall task is in one person's set of job responsibilities, that person doesn't have to write all the content by himself or herself. Give the coordinator the authority to assign everyone in your organization the job of creating content, even if it's only one 500-word (or equivalent) article per month. This works well because the task is spread around and also because people have different sets of knowledge.

One of the important skills of the "person in charge" is to develop the existing talents of your stakeholders. If some of your staff are particularly interested and have higher level skills, you may put them in charge of writing more or longer pieces. Someone with a good "radio voice" might read the material for audio recordings. A staff member who enjoys working with PowerPoint could put together a slide show and record an audio to go with it. None of the content has to be the equivalent of a term paper done for school. It should be grammatically correct, accurate in terms of its information (of course!) and yet still of interest and comprehension to a lay audience. Depending on how many people you have on staff, how many volunteers you can get, and so on, you can develop a significant set of information-based content in a few months.

Action 2-3: Spread the fame.

As you develop the idea of significant content creation to make your agency famous, you will probably find that the staff, volunteers, Board, and maybe even your clients, would like to see more of the content creation become part of their assigned tasks. Most people enjoy the recognition that comes from having their "voice" put into the larger world. As long as there is some oversight of the content that goes out under the name of the organization or is posted on the website, the more recognition you can give the actual creator, the better. Let people specialize in their areas of knowledge, take responsibility for a topic area, and create content to their heart's content.

As an aside, it should be clear that, while the person who wrote the material is the author or the creator of the content in whatever form it is made, that copyright belongs to the organization and the material is "work for hire" or part of the person's job responsibilities. If created by a volunteer, it is important to transfer copyright legally to the agency.

Step 3: Be Current and "Evergreen"

In addition to generating a lot of high quality content, it is important to provide content which meets the needs of your target audience for both up-to-date information and content that is perennially relevant. The first type is "current content" while the second is "evergreen content". What's the difference, and why should you care? Current content attracts visitors who are trying to find information about relevant recent events and new developments in the field. Evergreen content is information that doesn't change—it stays accurate and relevant over longer periods of time.

Consider a substance abuse prevention organization. This organization can draw traffic (website visitors) interested in current content by providing a professional reaction to a local drunk-driving car wreck or high profile overdose, or by translating into common language a new research report revealing the latest trends in drug use patterns or a promising new approach to prevention.

Creating content related to current events lets your consumers know that you are in touch with your community and that you have an informed stance on new developments in the field. Special situations, such as holidays, breaking news and even staff birthdays can be a part of your content creation strategy. Just be sure the information is related to your audience's interests and level of knowledge.

Evergreen material (that is, content that is not outdated over longer periods of time) is also valuable because it will be information that is sought-after for a long time and is therefore more likely to be ranked high in the search engines. It also adds a sense of depth to your organization's website when you keep basic knowledge accessible to old and new visitors alike.

Current content is fresh. Evergreen content lends weight.

Just as a local fitness center can draw constant website traffic by maintaining basic information about choosing running shoes, counting calories, or rehabbing common injuries, so could a substance abuse center have information about what the effects of various drugs are, what common street names for drugs are, what the signs of alcohol and drug abuse are, and so on. This information, once written, will likely stay on your site or YouTube channel for a long time.

The content which is most consistently accessed by new visitors should become a permanent feature of your website, as long as it remains relevant. You should, however, regularly review all content on your site – evergreen content included – to ensure that it is still accurate and useful. Even longstanding information may change or become less sought after by your target groups. Assign someone to review the pages of your website regularly, at least every year, especially when new information that counters previously held ideas becomes available. We'll talk more about how to evaluate and adjust your content creation strategy later, in Step 5.

A mix of current events-related content and information that doesn't become inaccurate will make your total body of content both fresh and important. Having a mix keeps your visitors returning for the new and keeps your site seen as authoritative in scope.

Action 3-1: Plan ahead for current content.

Have you ever wondered how businesses find new connections to sell things? For example, would George Washington, Abraham Lincoln, Christopher Columbus, and Martin Luther King really approve of their birthdays being used to peddle products? How about the originators of Mother's and Father's days? Most likely not. But businesses know that these opportunities come around every year and they are prepared to put their wares on sale.

How about similar thinking for your nonprofit? Many alcohol and drug addiction treatment centers put out press releases around the December holidays to provide tips on dealing with grief at this time of the year. Shouldn't this be on their content creation calendar? Many topics have a "month" or "week" or maybe just a "day" devoted to them. These are just made up from the desire to bring awareness to a cause and you can create your own "name that topic" day. Here are some examples:

- February 1-28 or 29: Black History Month
- February 1-28 or 29: National Children's Dental Health Month
- March 1-31: National Social Worker's Month
- June 26: International Day Against Substance Abuse and Illicit Trafficking
- August 13: National Left-hander's Day
- August 26: Women's Equality Day

- September 15-October 15: Hispanic Heritage Month
- September 1-30: World Alzheimer's Month
- Last Wednesday in September: National Women's Health and Fitness Day
- October 1-31: National Breast Cancer Awareness Month
- October 10: Mental health day
- October 10: World Homeless Day
- October 13: Metastatic Breast Cancer Awareness Day
- November (2nd full week): National Hunger and Homelessness Awareness Week
- December 1: World AIDS Day

Not every nonprofit agency will easily fit into each of the "days", "weeks", or "months" but if you use your imagination, you may find ways to genuinely contribute to bringing awareness about serious issues. In this way you can plan current content.

Action 3-2: Current content can come from anywhere.

While it is useful to plan ahead for current content, you will want to be respectful of other organizations' topics. But you can create current content from a wide variety of things: Your CEO's birthday, a fundraiser for your organization that is bringing in a well-known speaker, the special achievements of a client, a speech made by a member of city council, a bill being proposed by the state legislature (don't run afoul of lobbying laws, though), or even a new movie coming out.

Action 3-3: Keep evergreen content stockpiled.

One great tip to keep in mind as you create content is that evergreen content can be kept stockpiled. That is, you can have people create content that won't go out of date and keep it until you don't have any current content and it's time to post, tweet, upload or otherwise release content according to your overall schedule. This means you don't have to be anxious about having nothing to provide because there is you always have something in reserve. If a current content piece comes up in the meantime, because the evergreen content is not time sensitive, you can use the current events-related content and save the other.

Step 4: Create Variety

In order to ensure wide distribution of your web content, it is important to format your information in a variety of ways so that your content is relevant across different platforms. Not all visitors want to read a long page about each topic you wish to share. Consider alternative ways to display information in attention-grabbing forms, such as:

- Blog posts
- Photographs
- Infographics
- Cartoons
- Videos
- Presentations
- Podcasts
- White papers and research results

Becoming Famous

You have the opportunity to package information in multiple forms. You could, for example, write a white paper, discuss it on a podcast, create a PowerPoint presentation to upload from the white paper, turn that into a video, and put the data results into an infographic. Now, the information in your original white paper has been repurposed many times, is still interesting and has become accessible to a wider range of consumers because you shared it appropriately in different venues! An infographic or an arresting photo makes a great addition to your Instagram page. A heartwarming or funny video may travel far via Facebook shares.

Remember that it is useful to vary the style of the content you create and share. Your material doesn't always have to be serious and "professional." Good-natured humor is more likely to be shared on social media than is factual data. When you set up your content creation plan, incorporate variety into your approach. Notice what catches your own eye when you spend time online and find ways to share information similarly.

Action 4-1: Use all your senses when you plan and develop your content.

People experience the world in different ways. Some prefer to gather new information through reading, some by listening, others by "doing". While it is unlikely you'll be able to include taste and smell in your content, you can appeal to the nose through vivid writing and images that access your consumer's olfactory senses. Give yourself the challenge of including all of the senses when it comes to creating content.

Becoming Famous

A sense that is often overlooked in preparing content for a nonprofit is the sense of humor! A witty blog post, a funny cartoon, or a wry remembrance told during a podcast can stay in a person's mind a long time, assisting your organization in losing its invisibility quickly. Apparently, when you're using YouTube as a way to disseminate information, having a cat in your video increases the odds of the video going viral and being seen by millions of people. Wouldn't that be a wonderful way to become famous!

Action 4-2: Include a variety of viewpoints in your content.

Nonprofit staff members who are adopting a content creation strategy to increase their organization's profile have a lot of work to do on top of their regular work helping clients, running the agency, raising funds and so on. Sometimes, the stress of doing more leads to a sort of "easiest way out" mentality which can also lead to having only one viewpoint presented. While it isn't necessarily a good thing to undercut one's own position with contrary opinion, it can be a very good idea to present information that may be at least somewhat controversial or contradictory to the organization's position.

Opening up the type of content presented in this way is sure to get some eyes on it just for the novelty of the concept, as well as the true contest between viewpoints. Seldom is there only one clearly correct viewpoint. Being able to show the strengths of one's own case and the weaknesses of another's increases respect for the organization and person behind the viewpoint. This is another way of adding variety.

Step 5: Measure and Discuss Your Achievements

One of the best times in any nonprofit's existence is when it finally has captured "hard data" showing how much it has achieved, not just for itself, but mainly for its clients. This thrill of victory lifts morale, excites volunteers and provides the basis for future funding requests. The same can happen when you show that your content creation strategy has paid off with increased reputation, more volunteers, higher donations, and fewer potential clients not receiving services.

Sadly, unless you prepare for this day well in advance of when the reckoning occurs, you won't have the data to show that your efforts were well-worth the time and energy used. If you don't have a starting point measurement, few people are going to accept that there has been a change.

The best way to gather the needed information is to install analytics software to run on your webpages. While the term "analytics" sounds pretty "tech geeky" and perhaps even expensive, the fact is that you need to measure a number of things as you start your content creation strategy to becoming a less invisible and more famous organization. Analytics software will collect this information for you in the background.

Some such software is expensive and probably overwhelming to learn how to deal with There is, however, a free version that can tell you dozens of things that will help you know whether your efforts are paying off or not. It is called "Google Analytics." Google Analytics is one of the most used free applications to help you know how your online visitors are reacting to what they see on your site. While you probably won't want to do the technical work to allow the tracking yourself, it is quick for your webmaster to do so. In fact, it may already be done.

What you most likely don't know is what benefits you can get from looking at the analytic information.

The Google analytics tool has valuable untapped benefits.

There are many metrics that tell you who your content is reaching and how readers are reacting to it. Here are just a few of the very basic statistics you can get quite easily.

- The total number of visitors
- The number of unique visitors
- The source of the traffic
- How many cumulative pages are viewed
- How long a visitor stays on particular pages
- How many times visitors use social media to share your content

All of these numbers mean something important to your nonprofit as you seek to gain more visibility in your area of service and expertise. Be sure to have your webmaster collect this information, tell you about it, and, most importantly, help you figure out if you are meeting the goals you set out to achieve in the first place.

As people arrive at your website, it is very important to have an easy and quick way to search for information that is not on the home page. It is imperative to have a search box feature so visitors don't need to hunt all over your site for the information they want.

It is also very good to have embedded links in your content that go directly to other pages that define terms, provide additional information on related topics, and so on. These links help keep the reader on your site and build your reputation as "the" place to learn about topics of interest to visitors.

Action 5-1: Determine what you want to know about your content creation strategy for losing your invisibility and increasing your fame.

As you can see from the list of things that Google Analytics can tell you, it is a powerful piece of software. But rather than trying to do everything all at once, it is better to focus on a few key metrics that you can achieve (or at least work towards achieving) over a period of months. Still, if you don't know what you want to accomplish, it is doubtful you will make strides in any direction.

This action is a strategic one that requires you to do some investigation about what the data can tell you. Confer with others who can help make this decision, particularly if you're not sure what some of the terms mean.

Action 5-2: Choose and have your analytics software installed.

It's probably better that you don't do this yourself, unless you are pretty accomplished with website development and maintenance. But you *are* the person who can determine what information needs to be collected, analyzed and interpreted for further action. While Google Analytics is free, it does have some drawbacks, such as Google wanting to have access to your back-end information. While I can find information on both free and paid analytics software at the time of this writing, by the time you read this action step, the information would likely be out of date. Work with your web support person or team to determine the best software application for your organization's needs.

Action 5-3: Interpret what the information tells you and share it with your stakeholders.

It doesn't make any sense to go through the first two actions for this chapter if you're not going to take a look at the information that has been collected. Naturally, the data won't necessarily tell you much by itself and will need to be interpreted in comparison with the goals you set for your organization's content creation efforts.

Once you feel that you have clearly understood the data and can explain the results to others, it is time to let everyone else know the extent of success and the areas where further work is needed. Just as the creation of content has been a team effort, so should the celebration of successes and the commiserations if things have not gone as well as hoped for.

Becoming famous doesn't really happen overnight, at least not often. When you accept the advice given in this report, you also accept the idea that fame should be earned, not manufactured. It should be the result of hundreds of decisions, all leading to large quantities of high quality content that will assist and/or entertain those who come into contact with it.

Wrap-up and Summary

We've presented five key steps to enhancing your organization's online profile and raising your visibility. You've learned 15 practical actions to take to implement those steps. You now know that taking on a content creation strategy to losing your invisibility and achieving fame means greater recognition of your work, increased attention from foundation executives and thought leaders, and expanded access to potential donors and volunteers looking for somewhere meaning to contribute. Remember, as a nonprofit organization, "fame" means more opportunities to serve your clients, because you are recognized as being among the best in your field.

As a review, here are those five steps and 15 actions to "losing your invisibility and becoming famous" among the stakeholders you care about most:

Step 1: Create a plan for enhancing your internet presence

Action 1-1: Determine what you want to be known for

Action 1-2: Develop content about these terms

Action 1-3: Put your content on your website and spread links to your new content to your contacts and other dissemination venues

Action 1-4: Spread the word and get backlinks to your material

Step 2: Produce both quality and quantity of content

Action 2-1: Make it someone's job

Action 2-2: Make it everyone's job

Action 2-3: Spread the fame

Step 3: Stay current and also use evergreen information
> *Action 3-1*: Plan ahead for current content
> *Action 3-2*: Current content can come from anywhere
> *Action 3-3*: Keep evergreen content stockpiled

Step 4: Publish content in a variety of forms
> *Action 4-1*: Use all your senses when you plan and develop your content
> *Action 4-2*: Include a variety of viewpoints in your content

Step 5: Track your progress and adjust accordingly
> *Action 5-1*: Determine what you want to know about your content creation strategy for losing your invisibility and increasing your fame
> *Action 5-2*: Choose and have your analytics software installed
> *Action 5-3*: Interpret what the information tells you and share it with your stakeholders

As we've said from the start, using a content creation strategy to lose your invisibility and become famous is not a quick journey. It may be something that has never occurred to you, your board, your staff or anyone else in your organization. After you've read this report, though, we hope you are convinced that there are many benefits—more volunteers, more donors, and more exposure to foundations and clients — to having your name out there in the world. If you follow the steps provided here, we are convinced that, with time, you'll reap those benefits. Give the process time, and let us hear how things have gone for you!

BONUS Section: Maximizing Your Fame with Social Media Platforms

This section has been added to bring additional information to the content creation strategies described already. We add a bit of information on using social media to accelerate and maximize the rate at which you will see an effect from your efforts. After a brief discussion about why to include social media strategies, you'll see nine tips to use three of the currently most popular social media outlets (Facebook, Twitter, and LinkedIn) in ways to spread your content faster. This way you'll more quickly gain all the benefits of losing invisibility and becoming known to donors, volunteers, foundations, clients and the media. Of course there are other social media platforms (YouTube, Pinterest, and Instagram are just three), but those are not covered in this CAN-DO report.

Why Use Social Media to Share Your Content?

So far in this report, the emphasis has been on getting content onto your organization's website. This *IS* vital because this is where search engines are most likely to find what you've created. Still, each social networking site has millions of users. If you employ the right strategies when using each of these networks, you will be able to reach countless target audience members. This expands your content reach far wider than you might ever imagine. Take note that these target customers are not only confined in one location. These social media users are scattered all over the world.

Becoming Famous

You need not spend a hefty amount of money for this particular type of online marketing strategy. Most of these platforms are free. All you have to do is create an account, build your profile and start posting photos, content and videos about your agency and the information you have created. You really can't get a more cost effective approach to increasing your content outreach efforts.

In general, we know that potential volunteers, donors and other funders check out your website very carefully, but they also like to get a sense of the organization through social media sites and interactions. With the level of personalization allowed on these sites, you can use it to connect to your stakeholders in ways that are different than a traditional website approach. In the long run, you may even ask for feedback, post surveys, and answer questions asked by your existing and potential clients and other stakeholders.

You will also get to enjoy faster information dissemination than relying on a website-based content strategy. Having a great website filled with evergreen and current content is an essential foundation, as described earlier. Still, since millions of people use social media, you can see how your content can be distributed more quickly through social media than would otherwise occur.

Three Tips for Facebook

1. **Have a Facebook page!** This seems obvious, but too many organizations see it as an unnecessary and time-consuming use of personnel. But if you've come this far and are using a

content creation strategy to become better known, it would be a real waste of time not to use this and other dissemination platforms.

2. **Have a strong call to action.** Request people to "like" and "share" your posts and your page. People generally need to be directed to take actions like this but are happy to do so when it is asked of them. The amount of effort on their part is tiny but the impact on your organization's reputation can be quite large. This is definitely an important way to lose invisibility.

3. **Respond in a timely way.** People who post to your Facebook page generally expect to have an interaction with your organization. The pace at which Facebook moves is extremely fast—so you can't just look in once or twice a week and expect people to keep checking your page.

Three Tips for Twitter

1. **Understand the way that 140 characters can tell a lot!** Twitter gets denigrated by people who don't really see the value of a short posting such as "Eating lunch now. Good food at Joe's Diner". For an organization, though, it can be a super way of connecting with supporters, volunteers and donors. "Volunteers needed for 1 hour on Sunday at 2 pm. Show up, no preregistration needed. More info @ www.agency.org/volunteersneeded ". This Tweet could get all the volunteers needed without a great deal of effort. Of course,

you'd want to send reminder Tweets a day before and a couple of hours before, but this is much easier than needing to make phone calls or even than sending emails out (although that is another strategy to use as well). [Because website addresses can take up a lot of characters, Twitter automatically changes the links in your tweets to 22 characters (even if they are shorter to begin with) so you have only 118 characters to work with.] When you want to share new content with your followers, you can send a tweet with the link to the product (report, video, podcast, etc.)

2. **Understand how to use hashtags (#) appropriately.**
Hashtags are a way of indexing or providing key words to your tweets so that they can be found by others. For example, an organization might use a hashtag and its name or commonly accepted abbreviation so that people can search for the latest news or commentary about it. For example, the University of Texas at Arlington (UTA) might categorize a tweet with #uta . Keep your hashtag category something that can easily be connected to your agency. Be sure to publicize your Twitter account and hashtag so people will "follow" you and receive your messages.

3. **Follow others.** Often, when you sign up to receive the tweets of others or some other organization, they will follow you back. This means that they may forward your tweets to their followers, increasing the reach of your efforts. Be willing to

re-tweet for others so they will do that for you, too. Don't follow too many others too quickly, as Twitter may see this as suspicious activity by spammers. Go slowly and build up your base in a responsible way.

Three Tips for LinkedIn

1. **Create a LinkedIn business profile.** LinkedIn provides you with a free business page where you can post information just like your website. It is a good place to put content that is also available elsewhere because LinkedIn attracts more of a business-minded group of users, compared to Facebook, for example. Make sure to write this profile from the standpoint of a potential volunteer or donor—what benefits can you provide the reader who might like to know more or become involved with your nonprofit?
2. **Join already existing groups that match your organization's interests.** LinkedIn has thousands of pre-existing groups that cohere around similar interests. Use the search function to find them. Two groups that may be of interest to you are Nonprofit Leadership Alliance and Social Media for Nonprofit Organizations. Here you can interact with others who have similar interests and can help you spread your content when you post to that LinkedIn group.
3. **Reach out to others.** All social media outlets rely on the participants to, well, participate, if they are to receive benefits from the effort. Don't expect others to do all the outreach—get yourself

known by being out there with your content. Share links to your information, mention when you post new products, and read what others say as well. If you're seen as only wanting to help yourself, other LinkedIn users will ignore what you have to say.

You now have nine tips covering three giant social media platforms. These three platforms will multiply your efforts in losing your invisibility and becoming famous. While a website is the foundation of a content creation strategy, Facebook, Twitter, and LinkedIn are all powerful helpers to get your organization to be well-known and visible. Incorporate them slowly, but do move forward with this content creation approach to achieving fame.

Additional Written Resources

If you've found the information in this report intriguing, be sure to look carefully at the next pages to find out more about CAN-DO and what some of CAN-DO's other information products are. Each book, report and video addresses one or more ways you can bring new ideas to your organization, improve skills, build knowledge and solve problems. You owe it to yourself to sign up at no cost on the email list to receive notifications on the latest products that will help you lead a better organization. Go to www.uta.edu/can-do to sign up now. When you do this, you'll gain access to a valuable exclusive report, available for free ONLY to CAN-DO subscribers.

This report is one in a series written by Dr. Rick Hoefer and Shannon Graves. They are available for Kindle e-readers and as print-on-demand soft-cover books. Below are links to www.Amazon.com to read about and order other reports that are currently available:

Old Organizations, New Tricks: Five Practical Keys for Unlocking a Learning Organization by Shannon Graves and Dr. Richard Hoefer. Order from Amazon.com here:
http://tinyurl.com/OldOrgNewTricks

Summary: This #1 bestselling social work book provides the right amount of information to assist your colleagues, your board, and your organization to approach each day as an opportunity to get better, to improve, and to learn! This book, while short and easy to understand, will be your step-by-step companion on an exciting journey to becoming a visible and famous organization.

Your Organization's Riveting Story: How to Write so that People Read, Remember and Respond by Dr. Richard Hoefer and Shannon Graves. Order from Amazon.com here:
http://tinyurl.com/YourOrgRivetingStory

Summary: Too many nonprofit, human services and social work organizations have reports that are boring. This report will help you write an original, expressive, and downright riveting story about your organization. A riveting report will be read, remembered and responded to, with greater involvement and more donations.

From Group-work to Team-Work: How to Turn a Group Experience into a Great Experience by Shannon Graves and Dr. Richard Hoefer. Order from Amazon.com here:
http://tinyurl.com/GroupWorktoTeamWork

Summary: This research-based report simplifies and summarizes the most important principals of using teams in the workplace. Readers will come away with the knowledge needed to transform the way groups work in their organizations. The report provides a brief overview of the factors that affect team performance and the most common challenges that groups face when they come together. Most importantly, you will learn practical solutions – news you can use – for turning your work group into a coordinated, communicative, and successful team.

Can We Do Something More for You?

CAN-DO! The Center for Advocacy, Nonprofit and Donor Organizations [CAN-DO] is the nonprofit research and capacity-building arm of the School of Social Work, University of Texas at Arlington. We are committed to working with nonprofits to help achieve higher levels of excellence and positive client outcomes.

We are self-supporting through developing mutually beneficial contracts with our nonprofit organizational clients. Initial consultations are always free and we work diligently to keep your investments in our services as low as possible.

For your free consultation, contact Dr. Rick Hoefer by email at rhoefer@uta.edu to begin a conversation about increasing the capacity and visibility of your organization. Dr. Hoefer is the Roy E. Dulak Professor in Community Practice Research at the School of Social Work at the University of Texas at Arlington. He directs the Center for Advocacy, Nonprofit and Donor Organizations (CAN-DO).

Dr. Hoefer specializes in translating cutting edge, best practice research into usable practice points for organizations. His passion is helping nonprofits succeed in providing high quality services to our communities. He has over 25 years of experience working in and with nonprofit organizations, assisting them in improving their services through program evaluation, advocacy, and management consulting. Dr. Hoefer has authored more than 30 published journal articles and 6 books and has given scores of presentations in the fields of nonprofit management, advocacy, program evaluation and policy practice.

Shannon Graves is a consultant with experience in nonprofit management, fund development, strategic planning, and community organizing. She specializes in bringing best practices to service systems and organizations through the effective and innovative development of policies, programs, and people.

Becoming Famous

Learn More with Video Resources by CAN-DO

For timely CAN-DO tips and resources, subscribe to Dr. Hoefer's YouTube channel by searching for DrRickHoefer. You may also visit www.uta.edu/can-do for links to these highly ranked videos:

3 Ways to Raise More Funds Online:
https://www.youtube.com/watch?v=uwOBHV8JwLc

Decision-making Flow Chart:
https://www.youtube.com/watch?v=8ptq1SR0wok

Five Steps on How to Hire an Evaluator:
https://www.youtube.com/watch?v=hMEEBZJT4uE

How to Decrease Staff Turnover:
https://www.youtube.com/watch?v=GQqhsNsfWmc

How to Handle Nonprofit Mission Drift:
https://www.youtube.com/watch?v=m5Kwa8UnRIY

How to Use Grants.gov to Find Federal Grants:
https://www.youtube.com/watch?v=yDbGerr5Oek

Leadership and Learning Organizations:
https://www.youtube.com/watch?v=fdojiqAb9Ss

The Ethics of Advocacy:
https://www.youtube.com/watch?v=4x5PnVrt5zw

What Can CAN-DO Do for You?
https://www.youtube.com/watch?v=c8YR8ivyBPo

www.ingramcontent.com/pod-product-compliance
Lightning Source LLC
Chambersburg PA
CBHW070718180526
45167CB00004B/1531